SICHUAN PANDA FORESTS

Terri Willis

Technical Consultant
Dr. Devra Kleiman
Assistant Director for Research
National Zoological Park, Smithsonian Institution

RSVP

**RAINTREE
STECK-VAUGHN**
P U B L I S H E R S
The Steck-Vaughn Company

Austin, Texas

A production of B&B Publishing, Inc.

Editor – Jean B. Black
Photo Editor – Margie Benson
Computer Specialist – Katy O'Shea
Interior Design – Scott Davis
Contributing Artist – Barbara Hammer

Raintree Steck-Vaughn Publishing Staff

Project Editor – Helene Resky
Project Manager – Joyce Spicer

LIBRARY OF CONGRESS CATALOGING-IN-PUBLICATION DATA

Willis, Terri.
    Sichuan panda forests / Terri Willis.
        p. cm. — (Wonders of the world)
    Includes bibliographical references (p.) and index.
    ISBN 0-8114-6367-2
    1. Giant panda — Juvenile literature. 2. Giant panda — China — Szechuan Province — Juvenile literature. 3. Wildlife conservation — China — Szechuan Province — Juvenile literature. 4. Forest ecology — China — Szechuan Province — Juvenile literature. [1. Giant panda. 2. Pandas. 3. Endangered species. 4. Forest ecology — China.] I. Title. II. Series.
    QL737.C214W54 1995   94-41786
    333.95′9 — dc20   CIP
                                              AC

Cover photo
Giant panda in pine tree

Title page photo
A panda at the Assiniboine Zoo in Winnipeg, Canada

Table of Contents page photo
Forest panda habitat in Wolong, Sichuan Province

PHOTO SOURCES

Cover Photo: © George Schaller

Assiniboine Park Zoo, City of Winnipeg, Manitoba, Canada: 1, 10 left, 25 top, 40 both, 41, 45 right, 50 top
Chicago Tribune: 6 top
©Jessie Cohen, National Zoological Park, Smithsonian Institution: 7, 9 top, 37, 43 right, 45 top, 49
Courtesy of The Field Museum, Chicago, IL: 8
©1988 W.S. George: 9 right
©Zoological Society of San Diego: 36, 38 top
Courtesy of the San Francisco Zoo: 38 left
©George Schaller: 18 left, 24, 43 top, 46, 57
WWF/Stuart Chapman: 23, 56
WWF/Soh Koon Chng: 39, 47
WWF/Michel Gunther: 17
WWF/Mark Halle: 3, 32 bottom

WWF/Peter Jackson: 21 right
WWF/J. MacKinnon: 4, 16 left, 18 right, 54 left
WWF/Susan Mainka: 25 top, 26 right, 34, 42, 52, 60
WWF/Nancy Nash: 35 bottom
WWF/Tim Rautert: 14 bottom, 19, 22 bottom, 27, 58
WWF/Don Reid: 12, 15, 16 right, 30 left, 35 top, 50 right, 55, 59
WWF/George B. Schaller: 13 right, 14 right, 30 top, 48
WWF/Kay Schaller: 50 left
WWF/Kojo Tanaka: 22 left
WWF/Pu Tao: 11
WWF/Paul Wachtel: 53
WWF/Chris Williott: 44

Printed and bound in the United States of America.
1 2 3 4 5 6 7 8 9 VH 99 98 97 96 95

Table of Contents

Chapter One

Love at First Sight

Ruth Harkness and her guide, Quentin Young, captured a baby giant panda in 1936. The animal was known as a *bei-shung* (pronounced "bay shung") to the local Chinese people. It was the first giant panda ever captured alive and brought to the Western world. No wonder the whole adventure seemed like make-believe. It had been an amazing chain of events.

To begin with, Ruth Harkness was nobody's idea of a panda hunter. A wealthy dress designer, she liked to live among the splendor of high society in New York's glittering 1930s. In 1934, she married William Harkness, a sophisticated New Yorker with a taste for adventure. Just two weeks after their wedding, he set off for China, hoping to find a panda in the forests of Sichuan (pronounced "SISH wan") Province.

Set on mountain slopes, the forests of Sichuan are home to giant pandas. In the 1930s, no one in the Western world had ever seen a giant panda alive in the wild. Harkness wanted to capture a panda for an American zoo. Of course, the idea that Harkness's wife might go with him was unthinkable—women didn't do such things in the 1930s.

Unfortunately, William Harkness didn't succeed in making the trip either. Though he reached China, he was unable to get government permission to even enter the panda forests. After two frustrating years in Shanghai (pronounced "SHANG hi"), he died suddenly from an undetermined cause.

A Surprise Journey

In 1936, Ruth Harkness shocked everyone, including herself, when she decided to carry on her husband's expedition. She somehow managed to get the necessary approval from the Chinese government and set out on the expedition, assisted by Quentin Young and several local hunters who knew the mountains well.

Their party made the slow trek upward through the misty forest to an altitude of about 8,000 feet (2,440 m). It was November, and ice and snow made walking very difficult. Heavy fog limited their

"Then I too stopped, frozen in my tracks. From the old dead tree came a baby's whimper.
"I must have been momentarily paralyzed, for I didn't move until Quentin came toward me and held out his arms. There in the palms of his two hands was a squirming baby bei-shung.
"Automatically I reached for the tiny thing. The warm furriness in my hands brought reality to something that had until then been fantasy. No childhood fairy tale was more dreamlike, or more lost in a dim haze of make-believe."

— **Ruth Harkness in**
***The Lady and the Panda*, 1938**

Pandas live in the forests of Sichuan, Gansu, and Shaanxi provinces in China. Juizhaigou Reserve (left) in northern Sichuan is a protected nature reserve.

Ruth Harkness took Su-Lin to the Brookfield Zoo in Chicago, where the panda died after only 17 months in captivity.

vision. Thick stands of bamboo—the pandas' favorite food—covered the landscape and slowed progress. But Harkness persevered. Where walking was impossible, she crawled along the frozen ground. Finally, all her efforts were rewarded. After only a few weeks, she was holding a baby panda in her arms.

She named the male baby "Su-Lin" (pronounced "soo lin"), which means "a little bit of something very cute." He was taken to the Brookfield Zoo in Chicago, which Harkness felt was best able to care for him. From the moment Su-Lin arrived, a panda craze swept the United States. It was 1936—the country was in the midst of the Great Depression, and the adorable panda gave people something to smile about. Su-Lin's playful, clumsy ways had everyone under his charming spell.

Unfortunately, Su-Lin lived only 17 months in captivity. He was replaced by "Mei-Mei" (pronounced "may may"), also captured by Harkness, in 1937. A third panda captured by Harkness died on its way to the United States.

Tangier Smith, another panda hunter, soon acquired several pandas for European zoos. A new era had begun. People were no longer interested in seeing stuffed pandas in museums—they wanted to see living pandas. Many hunters and explorers descended on the panda forests, seeking pandas for zoos throughout the United States and Europe. Wild game hunters also wanted pandas for their personal collections. Giant pandas were shipped out of China as quickly as the hunters could capture them.

A History of Honor

Though giant pandas were new to Westerners, the people of China had known and loved these animals for thousands of years. Pandas had great mythic and historic importance in China. More than 3,000 years ago, the earliest collections of Chinese poetry—*The Book of History* and *The Book of Songs*—both mentioned an animal resembling the giant panda.

Giant pandas were also mentioned in the country's oldest geography text, *A Description of Mountains and Rivers*. As early as 1050 B.C., pandas were kept in Chinese zoos along with such animals as tigers and rhinoceroses. Panda skulls were buried in royal tombs with powerful emperors—truly a great honor. To the Chinese, the panda was a symbol of peace because it does not feed on any other living creatures.

Until 1869, no Westerner even knew such animals existed. Then Père Armand David, a French priest, visited a landowner in a Sichuan valley who showed him a panda skin. Père David sent the pelt to the Museum of Natural History in Paris. He later succeeded in getting four more dead pandas, which he also sent to Paris.

The Chinese used the bamboo-eating panda as a symbol of peace because it does not feed on other animals.

David gave the creature the scientific name *Ursus melanoleucus*, which placed it in the bear family. But zoologist A. Milne-Edwards, who studied the skeletons, decided that the panda was not a true bear. He named the animal *Ailuropoda melanoleuca*. This was a new genus classification,

Because it is so rare and so beloved, the giant panda was selected as the logo of the World Wide Fund for Nature—formerly the World Wildlife Fund—in 1969. The famous wildlife painter Sir Peter Scott, then chairman of WWF, designed the logo. Today, the giant panda is a symbol that calls for the protection of all endangered species everywhere. The WWF places special emphasis on programs to save its mascot, the giant panda.

indicating that the giant panda came from a family of its own, unlike any other animal. The name *panda*, however, was already in use. The Nepalese used the term to describe the red, or lesser, panda, a smaller animal found in the panda forests and other parts of Southeast Asia.

Suddenly a Target

Though American and European hunters immediately wanted to add the mysterious animal to their trophy collections, no one was successful for decades. The dense vegetation and heavy mist of the panda forests made hunting difficult for Westerners.

Then in 1929, the first panda was killed by a Westerner. Kermit and Theodore Roosevelt, Jr.—sons of President Teddy Roosevelt—hold this dubious honor. They simultaneously shot the first panda they saw. The animal's skin was sent to the Field Museum in Chicago, where it was stuffed and put on display. Several more pandas were shot for exhibits in various American institutions in the following years.

The giant panda is known by over 30 nicknames in China. *Daxiongmao* or "big bear-cat" is written in Chinese characters above.

However, several years later, the Roosevelt brothers were as charmed as the rest of the nation by little Su-Lin. After playing with the cute, baby panda for a short time, they vowed never to shoot another panda.

But plenty of other hunters were happy to catch giant pandas for zoos all over the world. Sadly, only 14 of 73 pandas that left China between 1937 and 1946 survived their journey to the Western world.

Pandas were killed and stuffed for museums in the United States. This exhibit was at the Field Museum in Chicago.

Handlers didn't know how to care for the animals properly. Pandas weren't kept in the right climatic conditions or fed the proper diet. No research had been done to determine what pandas needed. In 1949, the Chinese government finally set controls on panda exports.

These limitations on the export of pandas made

the panda even more valuable. Throughout the 1970s, the Chinese government used pandas as a political tool. Pairs of the rare creatures were given as treasured gifts—symbols of friendship—to such countries as the United States, Mexico, Great Britain, France, Spain, Japan, and North Korea. According to a document signed by the Chinese government, the panda was thought to be "not only the precious property of the Chinese people, but also a precious natural heritage of concern to people all over the world."

We Love Them to Death

Today, people still love giant pandas. In 1992, the San Diego Zoo offered $3 million to have a pair of pandas for three years. Attendance rises dramatically when pandas are on exhibit, and gift shops also sell lots of panda merchandise, such as stuffed animals, T-shirts, postcards, and books. The zoo's contract stipulates that all revenue will go for panda conservation activities in the wild, although zoo receipts will undoubtedly increase.

Unfortunately, the giant panda's popularity makes them prey for poachers, too. Panda skins purchased only for display sell for up to $10,000 in Hong Kong, Japan, and Taiwan. They make a flashy status symbol in homes and offices.

Because of poaching and other threats to pandas and the panda forests, the world's panda population has dropped by about 50 percent in the last two decades. Today, fewer than 1,000 giant pandas are left on Earth. Some experts think there may be fewer than 600. In any case, the species is in serious danger of extinction.

"That the panda has been enshrined as an icon of our environment is not surprising," wrote prominent zoologist and giant panda researcher George Schaller in *The Last Panda*. "The animal has the power to touch and transform all those who gaze upon it; it has only to appear to brighten a scene. Yin and yang are the two great Chinese forces of

Merchandising the likeness of giant pandas is always popular. This collectors' plate was marketed by the Bradford Exchange.

separation and unity: black and white, dark and light, sun and moon, summer and winter, life and death. Each force carries part of the other, each needs the other to retain a balanced whole with an emphasis on suppleness and endurance. The panda personifies this yin and yang. But humankind has upset the balance, and the pandas' existence is now shadowed by fear of extinction."

The panda's black-and-white markings personify the Chinese symbol of the principles of yin and yang shown above.

Panda Attraction

Researchers have tried to understand why humans are so drawn to giant pandas. We call some captive pandas by double names as a sign of affection. We follow news stories of their births and deaths, their mating, and their illnesses. No other animal rates this sort of tender attention.

Some people feel that pandas actually stimulate the human desire to nurture and parent. Pandas have some of the features that people find so endearing in young infants: big, round, inquisitive eyes; a roly-poly walk; a large face. We are instinctively programmed to respond lovingly to these traits, as nature's way of making sure adults care for their children.

Pandas don' t really have big round eyes, but the black fur surrounding their eyes makes them look much larger.

The truth is that pandas don't have the big, round eyes we are all so fond of. In reality, their eyes are rather small and almost shifty-looking. But the patches of black fur around their eyes make them seem large.

"Why do we love these creatures so much that visitors by the thousands will line up to look through a glass at a sleepy panda?" asked a 1988 *New York Times* editorial. "To watch a panda in action—waddling, somersaulting, munching bamboo sprouts, and heaving the occasional sigh—is to watch a child's stuffed animal come miraculously to life. That's precisely why children and their parents crowd the nation's zoos whenever one is exhibited."

Perhaps their scarcity is another reason we love them so much. A few mountain forests in three Chinese provinces hold all the wild pandas left in the world today. They live in just six defined areas that total about 12,000 square miles (31,000 sq km). Only a very fortunate few will ever see a giant panda in the wild.

A giant panda walks through the Wolong Nature Reserve in Sichuan. Pandas walk pigeon-toed, with their paws pointing inward.

10

Chapter Two

The Mountains of Sichuan Province

It is springtime in the mountains of Sichuan Province in China, and the forests are blooming back to life. The brilliant rhododendrons—pink, orange, red, and yellow—contrast with the rich greens of trees and bamboo. Flowering anemones, violets, crocuses, and wood sorrels dot the ground. Ferns push up through the rich humus of last year's plants, and new bamboo shoots appear. Red and blue sunbirds arrive after a winter spent in warmer climates. They are joined by orange and red tragopans, a type of pheasant.

The mountains are the focal point of Sichuan's spectacular landscape in southwestern China. Near the Plateau of Tibet, mountain ranges reach sharply skyward to frigid peaks above the lush subtropical valleys. Formed millions of years ago from sandstone, granite, dolomite, and limestone, the mountains rise up along the eastern edge of the Himalayas. Smoothed over thousands of years by wind, rain, and vegetation, the mountains are now a region of rich earth, supporting abundant plant growth and a variety of animal species.

Much of the fertile land, especially at lower elevations, is now covered by farm fields and houses.

The Qionglai Mountains rise toward the sky in the Wuyipeng study area of the Wolong Nature Reserve in Sichuan Province, China.

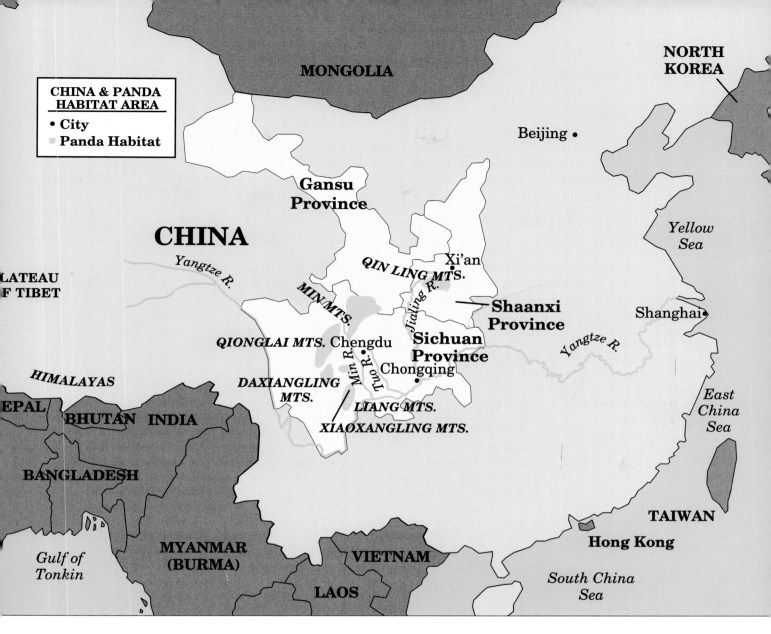

CHINA & PANDA HABITAT AREA
• City
▪ Panda Habitat

MONGOLIA

NORTH KOREA

Beijing •

Gansu Province

CHINA

Yangtze R.

QIN LING MTS.

Xi'an •

Jialing R.

Shaanxi Province

MIN MTS.

Yellow Sea

Shanghai •

PLATEAU OF TIBET

QIONGLAI MTS. Chengdu •

Sichuan Province

Yangtze R.

Min R.

Tuo R.

Chongqing •

HIMALAYAS

DAXIANGLING MTS.

LIANG MTS.

XIAOXANGLING MTS.

East China Sea

NEPAL

BHUTAN INDIA

BANGLADESH

TAIWAN

Hong Kong

Gulf of Tonkin

MYANMAR (BURMA)

VIETNAM

LAOS

South China Sea

Most of the remaining panda habitat is located in the province of Sichuan. The provinces of Gansu and Shaanxi also have some protected panda habitat areas. The pink regions on the map show areas of panda habitat today.

More has been left bare, the result of logging to meet China's great demand for lumber. The wilderness area left on these mountain slopes is shrinking, but what remains is beautiful.

Plants Aplenty

Altitude determines where plants will live on the slopes. At the mountain peaks—18,000 feet (5,480 m) high or more—is the snow zone, where only a few lichens grow. Just below, the alpine meadow descends to a level of about 12,000 feet (3,655 m). Grasses grow here along with hardy plants, such as poppies whose large yellow flowers are regularly glazed with ice.

Below the alpine meadow lies a band of about 3,000 feet (915 m) where rhododendrons dominate, interspersed with a few fir and spruce trees. Next is

Beautiful rhododendron bushes bloom in the woods of fir and spruce.

the 6,000-foot (1830-m) band known as the bamboo forest. Here dense stands of bamboo cover nearly 80 percent of the ground. Overhead are taller trees, including maple, poplar, willow, birch, evergreen, spruce, fir, and hemlock. Again, rhododendrons add a splash of vivid color. Below the bamboo forest, deciduous and coniferous trees are abundant in the valley.

As part of its natural cycle, bamboo plants die after the flowers bloom. Different types of bamboo may bloom from every 35-40 years up to every 120 years.

A Simple Diet

Bamboo, a grass, is the foundation of the giant pandas' existence. Other animals may eat some bamboo, but only the giant panda lives on it almost exclusively. Just one percent of the panda's diet comes from other foods.

There are more than 40 types of bamboo, but pandas eat only about ten types. Within each giant panda's range, there are usually about three bamboo species to choose from.

Bamboo grows quickly, as much as one inch (2.5 cm) per day, up to a height of as much as 60 feet (18.3 m), though most are 15 feet (4.6 m) or less. Bamboo stalks measure from 0.5 inches (1.2 cm) in diameter to 1.5 inches (3.5 cm). The sectioned stalks are hollow, with hairlike nodes on the outside and slender, pointed leaves. Bamboo leaves remain green and stay on the stalks over winter, giving the appearance of an evergreen. The stalks are very dense, and visibility within a stand, or thicket, of bamboo can be as poor as 2 feet (0.6 m).

A panda can crush the tough outer covering of a bamboo stalk by using its strong jaw and large teeth. The softer material inside, called pith, makes a good meal.

pith

Giant pandas prefer to eat broken bamboo shoots (right) and bamboo leaves, but they also eat the stalks.

Bamboo has an unusual life cycle. The plants grow and survive without producing seeds every year. They multiply by sending out underground runners that grow upward into new plants each season. Bamboo plants flourish for periods of 15 to 120 years, then all the plants of a species suddenly flower, produce seeds, and die.

Eventually, the seeds fall to the ground and grow into a new stand of bamboo, but that process takes several years. Until then, giant pandas must find a new source of food either by switching to a different type of bamboo or by moving to an area where that species of bamboo has not died.

No one really knows why bamboo flowers and then dies, but one explanation seems likely. The tangle of bamboo roots under the ground may become so old, thick, and matted that they can no longer send out new runners. The whole stand must then die off to clear the area for the next generation of bamboo. The dead stand decomposes, enriching the soil for new bamboo plants to take root.

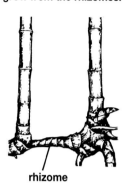

Bamboo reproduces by sending out underground stems called rhizomes. New shoots grow from the rhizomes.

rhizome

Live stands of arrow bamboo grow near dead stands of another type of bamboo in this forest in the Wolong Nature Reserve.

An Unusually Wet Place

In late spring, young giant pandas begin to explore their world. Pandas are surrounded by the mainstay of their diet—bamboo. Cherry trees come into bloom, and rosebushes flower. The sun beats down on the pleasant scene, but not for long. By June, the rains come and never seem to stop.

For most of the year the environment is wet. Winters are snowy, summers are humid, and heavy downpours are common. Winds carry moisture from the Pacific Ocean across the vast expanse of China to the mountains. The moisture condenses into rainfall and mist when it hits the steep, chilly slopes.

Following each rainy summer, autumn turns the forest into a vibrant mass of color for a few brief weeks. Birch and maple trees are gold and orange; dogwood and viburnum are scarlet before most leaves fall to the ground. But throughout the winter, conifers, rhododendrons, and bamboo keep their green leaves.

The frigid December winds carry massive amounts of snow. By February, hints of springtime warmth are in the air, and by April, the snow melts into rivulets that flow down the mountainsides. In the valleys, the snowmelt joins the waters of the Min, Tuo, or Jialing rivers (pronounced "min," "too," and "zha ling")—which empty into the great Yangtze River (pronounced "yang tsee"). The Yangtze carries the water to the East China Sea. From there, it goes back to the Pacific, and springtime is again on its way to the Sichuan mountain forests.

The Sichuan panda forests are especially beautiful in autumn.

Animal Variety

Giant pandas share the mountainsides with about 500 other animal species. So many types of animals live there because there is such a wide diversity of climates—from frigid mountain peaks to temperate forests, and valleys that are almost tropical.

The incredible variety of large animals makes China's southwestern mountains the most diverse mammal region in the Northern Hemisphere. But the populations of each plant and animal species are small. There are many different types of plants but not enough of any individual plant species to support a large number of one type of animal.

Altitude determines the climate on the mountain slopes, and climate determines where certain plants grow. All these factors—altitude, climate, and plant growth—determine where certain animals live. From time to time, the animals overlap into higher or lower regions, but generally each animal stays in its specific niche.

Chenshui Creek in Wuyipeng study area of the Wolong Nature Reserve rushes down a hillside surrounded by new spring plant growth.

Blue sheep, also called bharal, inhabit the treacherous high cliffs of the upper altitudes. Neither sheep nor goats, they descended from a common ancestor of both. They get their name from their grayish-blue hair. Also found in the alpine meadow are serows, a type of goat found only in Asia. Their smaller cousins, the gorals, can be found there, too. Gorals are agile climbers. Shallow indentations in their hooves act like suction cups, flattening out as they walk and helping gorals maintain their footing on the narrow cliffs.

Here, too, live beautiful snow leopards, rare creatures considered by some to be the most beautiful cats in the world. Their tails are nearly as long as their 4-foot (1.2-m) bodies, giving them superb balance as they move swiftly around the mountainside. Though they live mainly in the alpine meadow, they sometimes venture farther down the mountain. These leopards are predators that feed mainly on smaller mammals.

Few birds fly over the alpine meadow. Sometimes a small number of ravens will soar overhead, looking for leftovers from a snow leopard's meal.

Snow leopards, one of the most beautiful animals on Earth, are an endangered species. They live in the Sichuan forests, too.

Occasionally a hawk can be seen killing a mouse or a rabbit.

In the middle altitude—the bamboo forest—the giant pandas live with such animals as porcupines, civet cats, and squirrels. Another resident is the unusual-looking takin, a relative of the musk ox.

Weighing in at about 700 pounds (318 kg), takins look like overinflated goats. They have short, muscular legs with broad hooves that are 6 inches (15 cm) in diameter. Their large, stocky bodies are covered with coarse fur, and curved horns adorn their wide heads. Takins are found nowhere else in the world. They graze almost the entire mountain slopes—from about 4,000 to 15,000 feet (1,220 to 4,570 m), constantly munching grass.

Takins live in herds high in the mountains of Sichuan. Like the bighorn sheep of North America, they are sure-footed and can travel over steep slopes quickly.

Fierce wild dogs hunt in packs in the bamboo forests of Sichuan. Rusty-colored animals with bushy, black-tipped tails, they prey on small mammals and the young and weak of larger species—including giant pandas and small, solitary tufted deer. Other predators include Asiatic black bears, red foxes, weasels, minks, and badgers. Though there are several species of predators, their populations are small.

The forests are home to beautiful pheasants, too. Temminck's tragopan pheasant has stunning

ENDANGERED ANIMALS

Giant pandas are not the only endangered species in the mountains of Sichuan. Snub-nosed golden monkeys (right) and golden takins have also made the list.

The golden monkeys, like the pandas, are considered national treasures in China. Their long, silky manes of golden fur keep them warm even in the harsh winter months. The monkeys live in the trees above the bamboo forest but venture down to munch on bamboo, berries, buds, and leaves.

The golden takins, too, have golden fur, and large, rounded noses, humped backs, and unusual twisted horns that curve out and forward, then back. Though the takin population has been dangerously low, their numbers are growing again because takin predators—wild dogs and leopards—have been hunted in the Sichuan forests.

crimson feathers. When mating, males display bright blue horns that puff up from beneath the feathers on each side of their head, as well as a bright blue neck pouch they inflate. Monal pheasants are equally colorful, with shimmering green, purple, and blue feathers that glisten in the sunlight as they move.

Many other birds, such as woodpeckers, wrens, egrets, and indigo copper birds, also make their homes in the trees of the middle and lower levels. They share the trees with such animals as stump-tailed macaque monkeys and flying squirrels. Another type of panda, the red panda, also climbs among the upper branches of the trees.

The red panda, also known as the lesser panda, is a distant relative of the giant panda. Much smaller, it weighs only 8 to 10 pounds (3.6 to 4.5 kg) and is no more than 3 feet (91 cm) long. These agile creatures look like raccoons, with dark patches of fur around their eyes and long, bushy red tails with black bands.

Like giant pandas, red pandas eat mostly bamboo, but red pandas prefer the leaves, while the giant panda fills up on the stalks. In this way, the two species don't compete for food. Nature has made sure that both kinds of pandas get the bamboo they need. Their lives depend on it.

Although the red panda looks nothing like a giant panda, they are distant cousins.

Chapter Three

The Panda and Bamboo

Bamboo is nearly as important to giant pandas as air. They eat little else—99 percent of their diet consists of this woody grass.

Giant pandas live only where bamboo is available—they wander no farther up the mountainside than their food source, about 10,000 feet (3,050 m). Their favorite varieties are the umbrella, golden, and arrow bamboo, and they eat an astonishing 40 pounds (18.2 kg) per day. This adds up to about 3,000 thin stems or 700 larger ones.

Why is bamboo so important? Giant pandas have the ability to eat other foods—grasses, fruits, even small birds and mammals from time to time. And other foods are much more nutritious than bamboo. So why is the panda so dependent on it?

Prehistoric Pandas

The answer goes back to the Pleistocene period nearly two million years ago. Long before humans appeared on the planet, pandas were roaming around the tropical rain forest that is now a part of southern, central, and southwestern China.

At that time, giant pandas were about half the size they are today—rather chubby creatures, good

"Much of what endears the panda to people around the world, from its roly-poly appearance to its docile manner, can be traced to the panda's unique and constant search for a square meal—the life of a hard-working hobo."

– Hu Jinchu, panda researcher, 1990

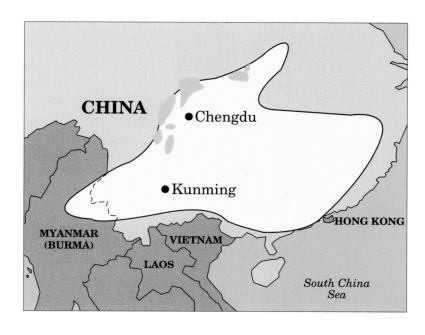

Pandas once roamed a large part of China as shown in yellow on the map. Today their range (shown in pink) is confined to a few areas in Sichuan, Gansu, and Shaanxi provinces.

tree climbers, but not too fast-moving. They were omnivores—they ate meat as well as fruits and vegetables—but their slow pace made hunting difficult. The pandas that found plentiful food sources other than meat were healthier and lived longer.

Bamboo was one alternative, but pandas had to eat a lot of it to get the necessary nutrients. However, in the humid rain forests where they lived, bamboo was always plentiful. The giant pandas that ate bamboo never went hungry. They survived, mated, and passed their preference for eating bamboo on to their descendants.

Over thousands of years of evolution, giant pandas adapted to a bamboo diet in many ways. Their body structure changed so that they could live more easily on bamboo, but these changes made the pandas even less able to digest meats and other foods. Their dependence on bamboo grew.

Custom-Made for Bamboo

Over many years, the sharp teeth of the giant panda became broad and flat—excellent for grinding bamboo stalks but poor for ripping animal flesh. Their faces grew more round and bulky as they developed powerful jaws well able to chew bamboo so thick and woody that even an ax couldn't chop it. As panda researcher Desmond Morris said in 1966, "The whole head has become modified as a crunching machine."

The giant panda developed a tough, thick stomach and esophagus to protect against any sharp pieces of bamboo it might swallow. The roughage, in turn, helps to clear out a fatty oil that builds up on the pandas' intestines and would otherwise block its digestive system.

Since giant pandas must eat such a huge amount of bamboo, they munch most of the day—nearly around the clock. They've developed an excellent sense of smell that leads them to bamboo even in the dark. The leathery pads on their forepaws help them grip the bamboo stalks. And one of their wristbones has become elongated into a pseudo-thumb that allows them to clutch slender stems with ease. They strip off and eat the leaves, gracefully peeling off the woody outer sheath of the bamboo. Then

One of the wrist bones of the giant panda's front paw is enlarged and elongated. It is used like a human thumb.

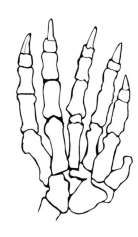

The leathery tissue covering the giant panda's forepaws helps it hold on to bamboo stalks more easily.

A CURIOUS FAMILY HISTORY

Are giant pandas part of the bear family or the raccoon family? The debate has raged for decades. A. Milne-Edwards was the first to give his opinion when he studied Père David's specimen and decided that it was more closely related to raccoons. That pronouncement settled nothing, however.

Recent studies of their blood show giant pandas to be more closely affiliated with bears. Other studies show that pandas' skeletons, muscular systems, and digestive tracts have several differences from those of bears. Giant pandas have shorter muzzles, more developed jaw muscles, and larger teeth than bears, along with the unique enlarged wristbone that functions as a thumb. And pandas make bleating, communicative noises that bears do not make.

Chromosome studies also point out differences. All bears have 37 pairs of chromosomes in each cell, except the spectacled bear, which has 26 pairs. Pandas have only 21 pairs in each cell. So far, scientists have found no definite answer. As George Schaller so clearly states: "A panda is a panda."

they munch the stem from end to end in much the same way as we eat raw celery.

Giant pandas have also evolved in ways that help them live successfully in the forests where bamboo grows. Fur on the bottoms of their hind-paws helps them grip ice and snow. Their round, chunky bodies are well adapted for chilly temperatures, and their thick, oily coats help keep them warm and dry. In the stark winter months, their black-and-white coloring provides camouflage against the snow and rocks. In the summer, the forest is so dense with bamboo that camouflage is not necessary.

Even the pandas' manner of walking was determined in part by their need for bamboo. They move

Pandas walk pigeon-toed, with the front legs stronger than the hind legs.

slowly on strong legs because they rarely need to flee a predator quickly in the dense forest. Though pandas may look fat and clumsy, they are really quite agile, and they need good coordination to peel the bamboo.

A Loss of Land

Giant pandas had already become dependent on bamboo during the late Pleistocene period, and they were thriving as a species. Then came the Ice Age. Huge glaciers reshaped the Earth southward from the North Pole. But the mountains in panda territory, more than 10,000 feet (3,050 m) above sea level, formed a natural barrier against the advancing glaciers and held them back. Areas south of the mountains continued to be warm and humid, so the forests remained thick and full of bamboo.

Guards in the Wolong Nature Reserve apprehend loggers who fell trees illegally.

Over thousands of years, glaciers advanced and retreated. In turn, the region's climate would shift for long periods of time from cold and dry to hot and moist. This played havoc with vegetation, including bamboo. After the Ice Age, bamboo covered far less of the land, and the giant panda's range was greatly limited.

Still, pandas survived the Ice Age. In recent decades, humans have proved to be a greater threat to the pandas' existence than the Ice Age ever was. Today, agriculture and logging are claiming forest-land that was once the domain of the giant pandas. And poachers are illegally hunting these rare creatures. But pandas still carry on their day-to-day lives in the wild much as they have for millions of years.

Each panda has its own scent, which is secreted from a gland under its tail. The scent is used to mark territory. Researchers study the pandas' scent posts (above) to learn more about each panda.

All Alone

Though they appear friendly, pandas are basically loners. The animals spend their days eating bamboo and resting. Each adult male has a range of 1.5 to 2.5 square miles (3.9 to 6.5 sq km). Young pandas and females have smaller territories.

Pandas mark their territory by depositing their individual scent. Large glands surrounding their genitals produce a sour-smelling, light-colored secretion. They rub their scent on trees, rocks, and logs. This doesn't prevent other pandas from entering their territory, but it serves as a warning. Typically, giant pandas avoid meeting face-to-face.

Pandas also avoid confrontation by using sounds to warn others of their presence and advise them to keep away! Researchers have counted eleven distinct sounds, from a roar and a growl to a bleat and a high-pitched chirp. Most of these sounds occur during the mating season. Pandas also snort or huff when they are angry or alarmed. They honk when they are slightly disturbed and bark when they are startled. Pandas squeal when attacked and roar loudly when they are being aggressive.

In most cases, pandas meeting face-to-face behave peacefully toward each other. Only during mating season do confrontations ever become

These Chinese researchers are inspecting the resting spot of a giant panda.

aggressive. Adult males may circle each other in an imposing fashion, or stare at each other, bobbing their heads. They may even swat or grab at each other, but little harm is usually done, although occasionally serious fights occur. Mother pandas can become ferocious when guarding their young.

Most healthy adult pandas have no predators. Occasionally, a leopard or wild dog may pursue a giant panda. When this happens, pandas can protect themselves quite well. They are slow moving, but they have powerful jaws for biting, sharp claws, large heavy forearms, and muscular shoulders for striking back. They can also climb trees if necessary.

Pandas have no specific nests or dens, though they often return each day to the same quiet, out-of-the-way place to lie down when they are tired. A female inhabits a den shortly before giving birth. She finds a spot in the hollow base of a large tree or in a rocky crevice. The mother then builds a nest of branches for the birth.

"THE BAMBOO BLITZ"

The giant panda starts its day at about 3:00 A.M., ready to search out bamboo and have a feast. The panda eats for about four hours, with peak munching time between about 4:00 and 6:00 A.M.

The giant panda eats in a very relaxed position, usually lying down or sitting with its back against a tree. Its forepaws are always free to hold the slender stalks of bamboo. When its meal is over, it takes a nap, resting against a tree trunk or a rock. Sometimes it makes a nest of bamboo.

Later it strolls around its territory, snacking on more bamboo, taking a drink of water from a spring or a river, swimming, climbing trees, and resting now and then. At about noon, it takes a two-hour nap, after which it sets out on another stroll, snacking regularly. All told, the giant panda walks about one mile (1.6 km) each day.

From about 4:00 to 8:00 P.M., the panda settles down to a serious supper with heavy bamboo consumption. It snacks, rests, and strolls a bit more before retiring at midnight for about four hours of sleep.

According to Chinese panda expert Hu Jinchu, all giant pandas follow this general schedule year-round, regardless of age or gender. Radio-monitoring collars placed around the necks of pandas have shown this to be true.

Mating Season

Panda females begin to breed at age five or six. Between March and May, they seek a mate, using vocal and scent signals to indicate their readiness. Males indicate their readiness to mate by depositing throughout their territory a secretion from their scent glands, which attracts female pandas. They also climb trees and produce a long, loud call to announce their presence.

Sometimes three or four males fight over a female. They may swing at each other and bite, but they rarely do any lasting damage. The strongest male usually mates with the female, and his genes are passed on.

After mating, the males go on their way. The female is again on her own to give birth and raise the youngster.

A giant panda cuddles her seven-week-old cub at the Wolong Captive Breeding Center.

Panda Babies

In late summer and early autumn—90 to 160 days after mating—the young pandas are born. Newborn pandas are not a pretty sight. At birth they are unable to see. They have sparse fur and no teeth. Less than 6 inches (15.2 cm) long, they weigh only about 3.5 to 4.5 ounces (99 to 130 g). Scraggly white hair grows on their pink skin. Their distinctive panda markings begin to show at about ten days, as patches of black and white become more defined.

Newborn pandas grow very quickly, however. By the time a panda is three months old , it weighs about 12 pounds (5.5 kg) and is 24 inches long (61 cm).

Mother pandas are extremely nurturing and protective of their cubs. They must protect babies not only from predators but also from the ferocious winter weather. They keep their babies warm by holding them in their arms and cuddling to nurse. Mothers lick their young to nuzzle them and keep them clean.

This four-day-old giant panda looks nothing like an adult. It has pink skin and very little fur. An adult weighs 900 times more than a newborn panda.

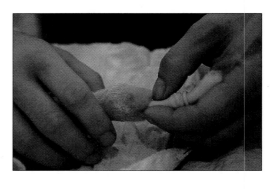

When the panda cubs are about two years old, they leave their mothers to find their own territory. Pandas are generally solitary animals.

Mothers do not leave their newborn babies for about a week. Then the young must be left alone in the den while their mothers go out in search of food. The babies are completely vulnerable to a host of predators. But when pandas are a few months old, they're covered with fur. This helps them withstand the moist environment, so they begin to accompany their mothers on trips to eat bamboo. Mothers hold the babies to their chests and walk with three paws. They cradle the babies nearby while eating.

Unfortunately, since a baby panda requires so much devoted care, a mother is able to care for only one at a time. About 50 percent of panda births result in twins, but usually the mother leaves one to die.

In the spring, the mother and offspring leave their den but stick together as they travel around their territory. The youngster explores on its own, but the mother keeps a close watch and rushes to care for her young panda at the slightest hint of danger. Females usually mate again when the cub is 1-1/2 years old, and the subsequent litter is born when the cub is two years old. At this age, the cub no longer needs its mother for guidance and protection. It leaves to establish its own territory.

Pandas have survived in this way for millions of years. It is only in the last century that humans have intruded into their world and brought them to the brink of extinction. Most experts agree, however, that the world's panda population could rise from today's 1,000 to as high as 5,000 by 2025 if drastic conservation measures were set in motion.

Growing enough rice to feed the huge population of China must be balanced with the need to preserve giant panda habitat.

Chapter Four

Human Threats to the Pandas

More than 5,000 years ago, the first crops—rice and millet—were grown in southwestern China. The people living there were among the world's earliest farmers. They used primitive axes to cut trees and brush, and scraped the land with crude hoes. They planted seeds and months later harvested their grain. They did not realize it, but they were performing one of humans' great accomplishments—reshaping land to make it meet their needs. This was the dawn of the agricultural age.

Unfortunately, the beginning of organized society for humans marked the beginning of trouble for the giant pandas. Large tracts of forest were cleared for growing crops, and pandas began to lose their habitat. Loss of habitat is still the most serious long-term threat to pandas.

Loss of Habitat

Over the past 5,000 years, agriculture has taken over much of the original panda habitat, though most of the damage has been done in the last 100 years. Woodlands have been cut down for firewood and for grazing. The high moisture and

"The panda is the symbol of hope for wild animals and their wild places. No other endangered species...has ever had such a high profile. Its survival, more than that of any other creature, will prove that conservation can work. But to date it has not.... All the millions of dollars, all the scientific expertise, advice, criticism, and public concern may not be able to save the panda. If it becomes the twenty-first century's dodo it will only prove what has been suspected, and perhaps known, for many years. . .there really is not a great deal of hope for any large wild animals on this planet."

— Clive Roots, zoological consultant, 1989

warm temperatures on the lower mountain slopes make them perfect for crops such as buckwheat, oats, beans, peas, and barley. As the pressure to grow more food increases, farmers move farther up the slopes, as high as 13,000 feet (3,960 m) in some places.

This agricultural activity places the farms well into giant panda habitat as bamboo is cut down and replaced with crops. This encroachment into panda territory has forced pandas to flee to higher mountain levels, or to narrow belts where bamboo still grows. Many pandas live in small patches of wilderness completely surrounded by human development. Since the animals come into conflict with humans when they travel through developed areas, most remain isolated on their small parcels of land.

Further damage comes when farm animals trample across the land and loosen the soil. Without the trees, the heavy rains beat down upon the loose gravel, causing landslides and serious erosion. Rich topsoil is washed down the mountainside into rivers and streams. Without the nutrients in topsoil, trees die. Also, the remaining soil cannot hold water from precipitation, so streams evaporate quickly during the dry season.

Farm animals such as water buffalo loosen soil, which can leave it more vulnerable to erosion.

Logging Danger

Logging also threatens the mountain forests. More than 30 percent of the forests of Sichuan Province have been clear-cut, or completely cut down, in the last 30 years. A great deal of this clear-cutting has occurred in panda habitat. Even though bamboo grows back quickly, clear-cutting of the trees can drive pandas away. They need trees to mark territory with their scent and to serve as birthing dens.

Even when clear-cutting does not directly affect bamboo, it can cause long-term damage. Bamboo seeds need cool, moist weather to germinate after a period of flowering and die-off. When trees are cut down, the ground is exposed to direct sunlight— making the soil too warm and dry for bamboo seeds to germinate and replenish the area.

At the high altitudes of the panda forests, trees do not grow back quickly. It may take 80 to 90 years for a forest of medium-sized trees to grow back. With cattle, sheep, and goats constantly grazing upon young seedlings, it takes even longer.

A reserve worker examines a stand of dead bamboo in the Wolong Nature Reserve.

Pandas' Greatest Threat

In most of Sichuan's panda habitat, less than 10 percent of the original amount of bamboo still stands, while other habitats have little more than a third. What does remain is quickly being lost. And loss of habitat is usually irreversible.

This loss of habitat can be particularly serious during a bamboo die-off. Throughout most of their history, pandas have adapted to the die-offs by migrating to another area of forest where a different species of bamboo is still thriving. But human encroachment means that there is less bamboo. And even when there is enough bamboo in another area, the pandas may not be able to get to it. They would have to travel through populated areas to reach it, and pandas avoid making such migrations.

Illegal logging in giant panda habitat is a constant threat.

30

Isolated Animals

With so little land still available to them, giant pandas cannot maintain large populations. Where only small "islands" of forest are available, pandas have splintered into small, isolated populations. Recent surveys have found fewer than 25 fragmented panda populations. Most have 10 or fewer animals; few have more than 50 pandas. These populations are usually made up of pandas whose territories are adjacent, perhaps even overlapping so that they are easily accessible to one another. When the forest is broken up by human encroachment, the panda populations become smaller, too.

AREA OF PANDA REFUGES: 1975 VS. 1989

PROVINCE	MOUNTAINS	AREA 1975	AREA 1989
Shaanxi	Qin Ling	936 sq. mi. (2,425 sq km)	438 sq. mi. (1,135 sq km)
Gansu, Sichuan	Min	5,135 sq. mi. (13,300 sq km)	2,369 sq. mi. (6,135 sq km)
Sichuan	Qionglai	4,044 sq. mi. (10,475 sq km)	1,370 sq. mi. (3,547 sq km)
Sichuan	Daxiangling Xiaoxiangling	502 sq. mi. (1,300 sq km)	237 sq. mi (615 sq km)
Sichuan	Liang	772 sq. mi. (2,000 sq km)	961 sq. mi. (2,489 sq km)
	TOTAL AREA	11,390 sq. mi. (29,500 sq km)	5,374 sq. mi. (13,921 sq.km)

Fragmentation can have serious long-term consequences for the health of the species. When their choices for mating are limited, giant pandas may face the problems of inbreeding and lack of genetic diversity. So far, these problems have been seen only on a limited scale among giant pandas, but they will probably become more devastating to the species in the future.

Inbreeding and Lack of Genetic Diversity

Giant pandas are solitary animals and rarely choose to come in contact with other pandas unless they are ready to mate. At this time, they must find a partner from within their own population.

Among giant pandas, the strongest males tend to mate with the females, either because they win the mating battles or because females choose dominant males. But today, since pandas are isolated in such small communities, inbreeding is increasing, and genetic diversity is decreasing. That means there is not a large selection of genes among the entire population. With less genetic diversity, giant pandas as a species may be losing their ability to adapt to new environmental situations. They are also more susceptible to disease.

Small populations lead to more inbreeding, which means that animals mate with their close relatives. Animals in the wild avoid inbreeding whenever possible, because the offspring of close relatives have less chance of survival. But in very small panda populations, inbreeding is unavoidable. Diseases and genetic defects can be passed throughout the population.

American biologist Michael Soulé, an expert on population biology, says that a panda population needs at least 100 members to remain healthy and vigorous over the long term. Currently, only about two populations meet this standard, and most of the others are much smaller. However, even the larger populations are seriously threatened by encroachment, and clear-cutting may soon separate them into smaller populations.

Poaching Perils

Next to loss of habitat, poaching is the most urgent problem facing pandas today, because it pre-

The government of China is trying to educate its population about the need to protect giant pandas and their habitat. The picture shows the entrance sign at Wolong Nature Reserve.

POACHING MUSK DEER

Musk deer are small creatures that prefer to keep to themselves. Only 3 feet (91 cm) tall at the shoulder, they hide in the forests, venturing out only in the early morning and late evening to forage for grasses and herbs. Male musk deer have no showy antlers, only long canine teeth that protrude downward between their lips, useful for scraping under snow for bits of food.

These creatures might have escaped the attention of hunters except for one special feature. Male musk deer carry a scent gland, called a pod, in a sac between their genitals. This pod, about the size of a chicken egg, contains a thick oil called musk, which is still used as a base for expensive perfumes. Each pod contains 0.9 ounces (25 g) of musk—worth more than $1,000. By weight, it is even more valuable than gold.

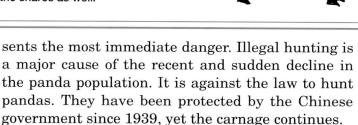

For centuries, these animals have been hunted for their pods. During the early 1900s, more than 60,000 pods were shipped each year from one Chinese port alone. All the perfume makers of Paris were eager to buy. In some years, more than 350,000 musk deer were killed. Today, only about 30,000 musk deer remain.

Musk deer are now protected under the Convention on International Trade in Endangered Species (CITES), which China signed in 1980. But though hunting the animal is illegal, the laws don't stop the poachers. Again, the potential for profit is worth the risk. Most musk deer are caught with snare traps, and other animals, including giant pandas, often meet their deaths in the snares as well.

sents the most immediate danger. Illegal hunting is a major cause of the recent and sudden decline in the panda population. It is against the law to hunt pandas. They have been protected by the Chinese government since 1939, yet the carnage continues.

In the past, local people usually left pandas alone. They were rarely hunted. Their furs were coarse and oily, their meat tasted rank, and they never harmed people or livestock.

Humans began to hunt pandas only in the last 100 years or so, when the value of panda pelts increased along with curiosity about the animals. Severe punishments are imposed for hunting pandas, but the threat of punishment doesn't seem to stop poaching. The potential for profit is too great.

An illegal skin can earn as much as $3,500 for the poacher from a dealer. This is a huge amount of money for people who live in the region. They don't earn much money, and the skin of just one panda can provide a substantial part of an annual family income. The skins are then sold by the dealer, mainly to people in Hong Kong and Japan, and the dealer gets up to $10,000 or more.

Some people want panda furs simply because

they are not supposed to have them—a well-known, though unattractive, human trait. In the 1980s, bear paws and the skins, antlers, and bones of many endangered species became very popular. The killing of these animals, including pandas, increased dramatically.

As more pandas are killed, the remaining animals become even more rare. This increases their value, encouraging more people to get involved in the illegal slaughter.

With these incentives, many people are willing to risk getting caught. There is a severe shortage of antipoaching patrols throughout the panda reserves and habitat, so most poachers are never punished.

In addition, many pandas are killed accidentally each year by snare traps set to capture musk deer. Poachers trap these musk deer at the same altitudes as the giant pandas, among the bamboo.

People Are the Menace

Some people suggest that bamboo die-offs are causing most of the giant pandas' problems. Indeed, there have been some serious die-offs in recent decades. Between 1974 and 1976, umbrella bamboo in the Min Mountains of northern Sichuan flowered

Villagers living in the Wolong Nature Reserve cut firewood to use for their daily needs.

Arrow bamboo grows at a high elevation in the Wolong Nature Reserve. An arrow bamboo die-off in the early 1980s caused many pandas to die of starvation.

and died. Nearly 140 pandas starved to death. In the early 1980s, arrow bamboo died off in the panda forests of the Qin Ling Mountains (pronounced "chin ling"). Again, many pandas died.

However, we know that giant pandas could survive the die-offs if humans had not taken over so much of their habitat. And more giant pandas are killed by poachers than starve during bamboo die-offs.

Human activities are causing most of the problems faced by the giant panda population. Humans are taking over their habitat and forcing them higher into the mountains or dividing their populations into smaller groups. People are hunting them for greed and killing them for their skins.

Other humans, however, are working to save the pandas. Several projects are underway in the hope that the species can be preserved for many generations to come.

This panda reserve sign reminds visitors and Chinese citizens to care for the pandas' habitat.

Chapter Five

Pandas in Captivity

"It is a sad irony that we who adore pandas also endanger their very survival."

— Hu Jinchu, panda researcher, 1990

A few sweet potatoes, apples and oranges, rice, a bit of meat—all these things are, from time to time, added to the bamboo diet eaten by Hsing-Hsing (pronounced "shing shing"). He is relaxed all day long, never worried about looking for more bamboo. It is brought to him regularly. And when he wants to, he sleeps in climate-controlled dens, never having to face winter's icy cold or the humid heat of summer.

Such is the life of one of North America's most famous giant pandas. Hsing-Hsing has lived in the National Zoo in Washington, D.C., since April 1972. He and his partner, Ling-Ling (pronounced "ling ling"), were gifts from the Chinese government to President Richard M. Nixon, commemorating the restoration of full diplomatic relations between the People's Republic of China and the United States after 23 years.

In December 1992, Ling-Ling died due to heart failure. Hsing-Hsing is still alive. He is one of the oldest surviving captive pandas in the world.

Life in Zoos

Considering the difficulties pandas face in the forests, many people might conclude that pandas are better off in captivity. We could put giant pandas in research facilities and zoos. There zoologists and other scientists can study them and find out what they really need for survival.

In captivity, giant pandas get nutritious food and excellent medical care. Captive pandas tend to have longer lifespans and therefore more years in

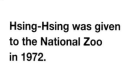

Hsing-Hsing was given to the National Zoo in 1972.

A giant panda at the San Diego Zoo (left) enjoys an apple instead of his usual diet of bamboo.

A veterinarian and two zookeepers give a health check to a panda at the San Diego Zoo. Two pandas, Basi and Yuan-Yuan, were loaned to the zoo from July to February in 1988.

The San Francisco Zoo had a popular panda exhibit from November through January 1985. Yun-Yun (above) and Ying Xin were loaned from the Beijing Zoo for a fee of $250,000.

which to produce young. Special breeding programs make every effort to help the pandas mate successfully. In the case of a twin birth, the second baby, which would be left to die in the wild, is cared for by humans. So far, though, only two pandas have been reared by humans from birth.

And of course, thousands of people flock to see giant pandas, giving zoos a good opportunity to teach people about the plight of the giant panda and what can be done to help. When Yong-Yong (pronounced "young young"), a 187-pound (85-kg) giant panda, visited the Bronx Zoo in New York in the late 1980s, she drew 2,000 visitors per hour.

In late 1993, there were 113 giant pandas in zoos and research facilities around the world, including about 90 in China. More than one of every ten pandas lives out its life in captivity.

Many giant pandas are on permanent exhibit, though the Chinese government also loans pandas, for a fee, to zoos throughout the world. China began lending pandas in 1984, when the government decided to stop presenting giant pandas as state gifts for permanent zoo exhibits. Giant pandas have been loaned to countries all over the world, including the United States. They have been on exhibit at such zoos as the San Francisco Zoo and the

Columbus Zoo in Ohio. The first pandas on loan went to the Los Angeles Zoo for display during the 1984 Summer Olympics.

There may be some benefits to keeping pandas in captivity. The World Wide Fund for Nature (WWF) maintains that a number of giant pandas must be in a breeding program in captivity to ensure the long-term survival of pandas. Jack Hanna, former director of the Columbus Zoological Garden, agrees. "A giant panda population must be established with a responsible breeding program in a United States zoo," Hanna said in 1993. Otherwise, "my personal opinion is that it is doomed in the wild."

But is it really beneficial to keep pandas captive? It's a question worth debating.

Money for Nothing

Keeping pandas in captivity and lending them out can be very profitable. The millions of dollars China earns from its panda loans is earmarked for conservation of panda habitat. But is this actually happening?

"The money hasn't gone back to China to protect the panda in any tangible way that we can see," said Ginette Hemley, a representative of WWF. "There's been no accounting system on either side—the zoos' or on the Chinese side—to show that this is indeed enhancing the survival of this species."

ARTIFICIAL INSEMINATION

Giant pandas have been conceived in captivity by artificial insemination. In this process, humans remove sperm from a male animal and inject it into a female animal in order to fertilize an egg. With this technique, researchers, such as those at the captive breeding center at the Wolong Nature Reserve (right), need not wait for a compatible pair of pandas to be located.

The first panda conceived in this way was born in Beijing (pronounded "bay ZHING") in 1978, and more have been born since. But much more research needs to be done before artificial insemination can be considered a truly successful method of captive breeding.

Still, a few conservationists are proposing a plan to use artificial insemination in wild populations of giant pandas. They want to capture some female pandas, artificially inseminate them with sperm from a panda of another population, and release them back into the wild. This would help reduce inbreeding and increase genetic diversity. But it would require constant human intervention, and many conservationists are skeptical of such a plan. Artificial insemination programs cannot solve the major problems facing pandas in the wild.

FROM CHINA TO CANADA

The Chinese government stopped giving pandas as gifts in 1981. Instead, they began the practice of loaning pandas to zoos around the world in 1984. The animals were used as goodwill ambassadors and to generate funds for panda conservation, research, and captive breeding activities. This "rent-a-panda" program was also beneficial for the recipient zoos, since pandas always create enthusiastic interest and bring big crowds. For example, after the panda visit to Toronto, Canada, the Toronto Zoological Society increased its membership from 5,000 to 25,000 members.

Eighteen zoos around the world have been privileged to exhibit pandas during the "rent-a-panda" program. One of the lucky recipients was Assiniboine Zoo in Winnipeg, Manitoba, Canada—and they hadn't even asked for the privilege. While on a trip to China, a local Chinese leader in Winnipeg, Dr. Joseph Yu, was asked if Winnipeg would be interested in having the pandas visit. After three years of planning and negotiation, a panda loan agreement was finally signed on May 28, 1988, in Beijing between the Zoological Society of Manitoba, the city of Winnipeg, and the Chinese government. For a $350,000 fee, two non-breeding pandas from the Chengdu Zoo, Rong-Rong (pronounced "Yong Yong") and Cheng-Cheng (pronounced "Chen Chen"), were loaned for a 4-month visit in Winnipeg in 1989. The pandas travelled in cages loaded in the passenger cabin of a Canadian Airlines jet. A veterinarian and zookeeper from the Chengdu Zoo attended the animals during the journey, monitoring their temperatures, their water intake, and making sure eager photographers didn't take too many flash pictures. Camera flashes stimulate pandas too much.

The visit was planned with great care, as the entire community raised funds to make the Pandas in Person exhibit possible. When the plane touched down on May 1, 1989, a sophisticated $889,000 building had been constructed to house the pandas. The outside enclosure contained 3,500 square feet (325 sq m) and the climate-controlled indoor enclosure added another 1,000 square feet (93 sq m) of living space. Scales were built in the doorway to monitor the pandas' weight each day. Besides the veterinarian and zookeeper from Chengdu, the Assiniboine Zoo had a keeper on call 24 hours a day. Security was beefed up, and 32 people were hired as interpreters and guides. The temporary zoo shop set up to sell panda merchandise earned $2,000 a day—that's almost as much as the Chengdu Zoo earned in a year in its gift shop.

Over 500,000 visitors saw the exhibit (right) before it closed September 5. Many participated in special educational programs designed to heighten their awareness of endangered species in general and pandas in particular. Besides the rental fee, all profits generated from the panda visit were given to the Giant Panda Breeding Research Base in Chengdu, as required by the Convention on International Trade in Endangered Species (CITES). Al Davies, head of Winnipeg's panda committee, summed up the success of Pandas in Person, "There hasn't been a negative about the visit. We really have to keep in mind what we did it for, the money that went to China, the facility left at the zoo, and the large tourist component...that brought people back to the zoo."

40

Conservationists also fear that the money the Chinese government receives from panda loans encourages officials to capture more wild pandas. Sometimes, giant pandas are loaned to zoos that make no effort to breed or study them. They use the giant pandas only to draw more visitors—and more revenue.

Giant pandas living in captivity do not have the freedom to roam like this six-year-old male panda in the Wolong Nature Reserve.

Leading Different Lives

Secondly, do zoo animals make good specimens for study? In a way, captive pandas are good specimens, because those in the wild are so difficult to find and study. Scientists have learned a great deal

about the biology and behavior of pandas by study-
ing the animals in captivity. But the lives of captive
pandas are quite different from those of their wild
counterparts.

Captive animals don't follow the same daily rou-
tine as wild pandas—they don't need to search constantly for bamboo. Instead, they are given the
bamboo they need to stay healthy. Captive pandas
also eat a variety of other fruits,
vegetables, grains, and even cooked
meat. While these supplements can
be nutritious, pandas often become
overweight, since supplements are
much more easily absorbed into
their body systems than bamboo.
Zookeepers must be very careful to
watch the pandas' weight.

In addition, we know that pandas are solitary animals who tend
to avoid each other whenever possible in the wild. In zoos, however,
several are often clustered together in exhibits. When pandas are
grouped like this, there are bound
to be a few shoving matches,
though they try to live in their
solitary way, barely acknowledging the presence of
others. But this forced togetherness in no way
approximates the life of the wild giant panda.

Captive giant pandas
are given enough bam-
boo and other food to
eat each day. Since they
don't have to roam in
search of food, they can
become overweight.

Captive Breeding

Finally, just how successful have captive breeding programs been? Unfortunately, few cubs born in zoos have survived. Most years, more captive pandas die than are born. One aim of captive breeding programs is to release animals into the wild. But captive breeding programs have not yet produced enough animals even to replace those in captivity.

Zoologists at the National Zoo tried to mate Ling-Ling and Hsing-Hsing, for example, starting in 1976. Finally, in 1983, there was a successful mating, and in the years that followed, the pair had five cubs. Unfortunately, all the cubs died, despite sophisticated medical efforts to save them. Two were stillborn. The others died within a few days after birth due to bacterial infections that overwhelmed their immune systems.

However, there have been some major improvements in recent years. The Chinese are producing more cubs and having more of them survive than previously. Prior to 1988, there was no more than one surviving cub each year. But between 1992 and 1994, 25 cubs were born, with 18 surviving. The Chinese have also developed techniques for hand-

Li-Li, a giant panda at the Wolong Research Center, takes care of her cub. China has had some success in recent years with its captive breeding program.

rearing cubs from birth, which should save another one-third of the cubs that die each year.

One obstacle to captive breeding still remains—the panda's mating behavior. Giant pandas, unlike most mammals, seem to be quite choosy in selecting a mate. In addition, most mammals can reproduce any time year-round, but pandas will mate only during one brief, specific period in the spring.

Even if a male and female panda are willing to live together, they may not mate. When captive giant pandas are kept in male-female pairs, if the pair is not compatible, mating is not likely to occur. In the wilderness, of course, the male panda has a larger selection of females from which to choose. And females in the wild may mate with more than one male during their mating season.

Cooperation between zoos with giant pandas must increase, so that a panda who is ready to mate may have access to pandas at several zoos. This will increase the likelihood of finding a compatible partner. The Chinese have organized a Giant Panda Technical Committee to achieve these goals. Chinese zoos now are more regularly exchanging and loaning pandas specifically for breeding purposes.

Hsing-Hsing lives at the National Zoo in Washington, D.C. He is the only captive panda in the United States.

The Present Situation

Conservationists are beginning to conclude that panda loans may also be a threat to giant panda survival. Some countries have taken notice. If the government of China would not change its policy, the other countries would change theirs. In 1987, the Swiss government became the first country to ban giant panda imports. The United States is tightening regulations and policy, too.

The San Diego Zoo in California, for example, had a $1-million area ready for the exhibit of two pandas. Plans were delayed in September 1993, however, and now the display holds only stuffed animals. The United States Fish and Wildlife Service called the halt. U.S. Secretary of the Interior Bruce Babbitt expressed concern that "the People's Republic of China may not be doing enough to conserve wild animals."

The San Diego Zoo had a giant panda exhibit in 1988, but plans for another exhibit were stopped by the U.S. Fish and Wildlife Service in 1993.

Rethinking Captivity

Keeping pandas in zoos is obviously not a natural way to save giant pandas or to preserve their native forests. "If we want to burden the panda with symbolism, reverence, and adulation, fine," said George Schaller in 1993. "However, we also have a moral obligation to maintain the species in the wild. With panda numbers dwindling year by year, not every zoo, not every country, can have them. The panda has not evolved to amuse humankind."

Captive breeding efforts may preserve the giant panda species, but the ultimate aim of any conservation program should be to preserve pandas in their natural habitat in China.

Some conservationists believe that captive breeding programs are necessary, however. "Despite the poor breeding record, there is a degree of security for pandas in captivity that does not exist in the wild where their numbers and chances of survival continue to plummet," explained Clive Roots, a zoological consultant who has studied giant pandas extensively. "Survival is the most important and immediate concern, but freedom should be the ultimate objective. Only the preservation of the pandas' wild places and the pandas' eventual return when it is safe to do so can ever justify keeping them in captivity."

As older pandas die in zoos, they are not being replaced. Many of us may never have an opportunity to see a panda. But our goal should not be to see pandas in zoos. It should be to preserve them in the wild. However, exhibiting pandas in zoos may be the only and best way to raise the money needed to save pandas in the wild!

A research facility at the Tangjiahe Nature Reserve north of the city of Pingwu is dwarfed by the rugged mountains. The high rugged mountains are not good panda habitat because bamboo cannot grow there.

Chapter Six

Controversies over Panda Conservation

When arrow bamboo began to flower in the Qin Ling Mountains in the early 1980s, people knew it would die soon. They had seen it happen with umbrella bamboo in the 1970s, when more than 150 pandas starved to death. This time, they were ready. The Chinese government prepared a plan to help save the lives of the giant pandas. Government forest workers and peasants alike would be paid reward money for each starving panda they rescued and brought to captivity.

Many people went to great lengths to help the pandas—one elderly woman even jumped into frigid waters to save a drowning panda. The animals were brought to special rescue centers where they were fed, sheltered, and treated for a variety of diseases.

The Chinese government took great pride in this program. A total of 108 pandas were captured. Chinese officials said that only pandas in trouble from illness or injury were captured. They helped only animals that would otherwise die. George Schaller disagrees. Most pandas rescued were not sickly, he said. Instead, his research showed that, left to their own devices, the pandas would have

The World Wildlife Fund works with the Chinese government to protect giant pandas. The picture shows a giant panda being transported to a research facility.

found enough food, as they have done for centuries without human help. Of those pandas captured, supposedly to save their lives, 33 died, 35 were moved to a different forest, and 40 were sent to zoos and holding stations.

Years after the bamboo crisis ended, the Chinese government continued to pay reward money, and the peasants continued to "rescue" giant pandas. It was a source of pride for them to be able to help the pandas, and the money was enticing, too. Most of these giant pandas ended up in captivity for the rest of their lives. What were they really rescued from? It was a program that began with the best intentions but ended up missing the point completely.

Similar controversies plague many programs that have been set up to help giant pandas. It's hard to know the best way to save the species and its forests, since the problems are so complex, and the time is so short.

Some pandas, such as this one at the National Zoo, have been "rescued," but that may mean a life spent in captivity.

Natural Reserves

China's Communist Party decided to establish forest reserves to protect wildlife in 1957 during the country's third National People's Congress. Another resolution five years later called the giant panda a "rare and precious animal" and declared that nature reserves would be created specifically for its protection. The environment within the reserves was to be carefully guarded to preserve the giant pandas and their habitat in every way possible.

The first panda reserve was established in 1963, the year after China named giant pandas an endangered species. Today, 14 panda reserves cover more than 1.3 million acres (525,000 ha)—about 25 percent of China's entire panda range. About half of all giant pandas remaining in the wild live within the reserves.

About 30 other endangered animals also live in the panda reserves, including the golden monkey, takin, snow leopard, red panda, and monal pheasant. Several thousand people live within the reserves, too.

WOLONG RESEARCH PROJECT

A massive effort to study and assist the giant panda took place at Wolong Nature Reserve over a five-year span, beginning in 1980. Additional research continues. The initial research project was a joint effort by the World Wide Fund for Nature (WWF) and the Chinese government.

Professor Hu Jinchu of Nanchong Teachers College, considered one of the top naturalists in Sichuan, led the panda research project at Wolong Reserve (above) along with George Schaller. The New York Zoological Society also provided major funding. At the time, Schaller was director of its conservation division—Wildlife Conservation International.

Researchers learned a great deal about the nutritional content of bamboo and how it is affected by the seasons. They also studied the pandas' exclusive taste for bamboo. They devised an emergency plan to deal with natural disasters, such as the sudden flowering and subsequent death of bamboo.

The giant pandas' behavior and daily movements were also studied with the use of radio-monitoring collars. Researchers defined problems in the environment that threatened pandas and suggested solutions. The main purpose of the project was to learn how best to help the giant panda continue on as a species.

Researchers spent many lonely hours tracking the solitary animals through the wilderness. They traced panda footprints (right) in the snow onto sheets of heavy plastic. By noting special features, they were able to identify each panda by its footprints. This enabled them to track the animals, learning where they ate and slept.

Since giant pandas are often difficult to spot, researchers also looked for panda droppings. They noted the location of the droppings, as well as the size and length of bamboo-stem fragments in a sample. The length helped the scientists determine the sizes of pandas in the area, since only the largest pandas can consume the largest bamboo stalks.

Much of the knowledge we have about giant pandas today was discovered during the exhaustive Wolong Research Project. But even that pioneering project is not without controversy.

Schaller's research was paid for in part by WWF, but he has criticized them for failing in their efforts to save the giant pandas. For example, says Schaller, WWF did not force China to help preserve the pandas in the wild by simply leaving them and their habitat alone. Instead, WWF spent money to build an expensive panda research and breeding facility in Wolong that is underused.

Representatives of WWF, however, say that this was the only way they could gain entry to China. While some of their efforts may have failed, they still have done more to protect the giant pandas than any other group. Not every attempt is successful, but at least they are trying to help.

Wolong Nature Reserve is, perhaps, the most important panda reserve. At 785 square miles (2,035 sq km), it is also the largest. Wolong is in the heart of the giant panda range at an elevation of 6,500 feet (1,980 m). Its annual rainfall averages 40 inches (102 cm), and its humidity is 80 percent. Arrow bamboo thrives on its slopes. With these optimal conditions, it also has the largest giant panda population among the reserves—about 140 animals were counted in the early 1990s. In addition, about 100 other mammal species and 230 bird species live in Wolong, along with 20 reptile and 14 amphibian species. Several of these various species are also endangered.

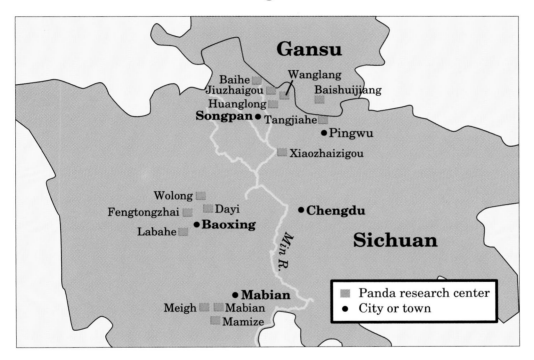

The government of China has established thirteen panda research centers in Sichuan Province and one in Gansu Province. New panda reserves and extensions of existing ones have been proposed.

The reserves sound like wonderful havens for wild animals, and to some extent, they are. Animals are safer in the reserves than outside them. But even in reserves, laws don't stop the killing. Wolong is not well guarded, and poachers still kill giant pandas for their pelts.

Also, forest clearing continues to go on at an alarming rate within the reserves. The number of people living in the reserves is also growing rapidly. They cut down trees for firewood and farmland, and continue to move higher into the mountains.

The Panda Plan

Today, a sweeping plan created by China's Ministry of Forestry to save the giant pandas offers some hope for the future. The Chinese Panda Conservation Plan, begun in 1989, is the largest effort yet to save giant pandas and is estimated to cost $100 million to implement. This plan was put together with the assistance of the WWF.

The plan's main objectives are to preserve wild pandas and their habitat; to restore habitat already damaged; to develop logging methods that will be less harmful to pandas; to improve captive breeding programs; and to learn more about what pandas need to survive.

Recently, the North American zoo community has also developed a plan through the American Zoo and Aquarium Association (AZA) to raise $30 million over 10 years to support the Chinese Panda Conservation Plan. It is hoped that a breeding population of pandas will be brought to North America as part of an internationally-coordinated panda breeding program, organized by Chinese zoo biologists. The request by the San Diego Zoo for a pair of giant pandas is now a part of this AZA effort.

These are major goals, and most are difficult to meet. But conservationists agree that these things must be accomplished if we hope to save the giant panda from extinction.

A six-week-old giant panda is cared for in an incubator at the captive breeding center in Wolong Nature Reserve.

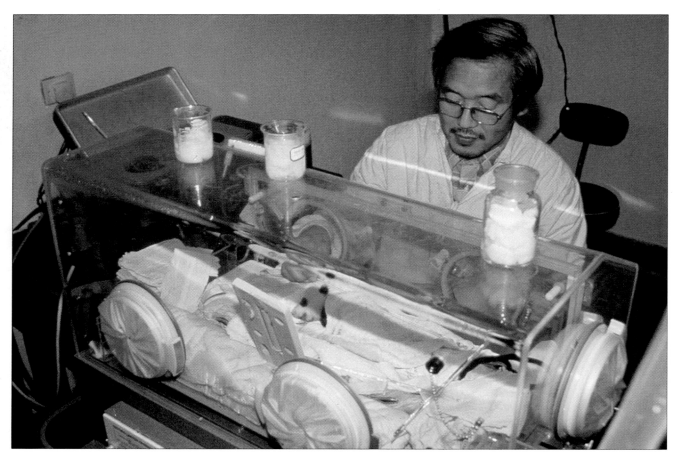

Homes to Save Habitat

In Wolong Nature Reserve, solid houses of brick and cement stand near a school, a hydroelectric station, and plenty of pastureland for grazing cattle. But most of these houses are empty. In fact, they have never been lived in.

Built in the late 1980s, they were part of the panda conservation plan. The government built the houses in parts of Wolong where pandas did not range. They hoped to move 3,000 Qiang (pronounced "chang") farmers of Tibetan ancestry who were living in the giant panda range into the houses. Trees would then be planted where the peasants had lived to restore the area to wilderness once again.

But the new houses were built in an area where farmland was quite poor, so most peasants resisted the move. Chinese officials eventually lost interest in the project, and tree plantings never began. The human population continued growing in Wolong—to over 4,000 residents in 1990.

This project was a failure. It was devised and put into motion based solely on the presumed needs of the panda and the government. Little thought was given to whether or not the people living in the Wolong area would actually want to move. "Any conservation effort must involve local people, based on their interest, skills, self-reliance, and traditions, and it must initiate programs that offer them spiritual and economic benefits," warned George Schaller in 1993.

It is difficult to get people to move in order to preserve giant panda habitat. The local people have sympathy for pandas and their plight, but they are in dire need of the land and resources themselves. They are not wealthy and must make do with what is available, including the land for farming and trees for firewood.

The human population continues to grow in areas near panda habitats. A Chinese peasant (above) walks toward his home in Sichuan Province near the panda reserves.

In addition, China's population is growing rapidly, particularly in the mountain regions. More than 100 million people live in Sichuan Province. China has a total population of more than 1.1 billion, and experts say that the population will reach 1.2 billion by the year 2000. More people need more space, and the mountains are among the few places left for expansion.

As China's population increases, the need for more land to house and feed them increases. By the year 2000, there will probably be 1.2 billion people in China, with approximately 1/12 of them living in Sichuan Province.

The Chinese Plan's Successes

Three-year-old arrow bamboo seedlings grow where bamboo had once died. Periodic bamboo die-offs encourage genetic diversity.

This example shows how difficult it will be to meet the goals of the Chinese Panda Conservation Plan. But there have already been some successes.

Most conservationists applaud the plan's approach to bamboo die-offs, for example. It says that the die-offs are a natural process that has occurred throughout time. Giant pandas have adapted to such die-offs and should continue to be left to do so.

According to the plan, no attempts should be made to genetically alter bamboo so that it does not have periodic die-offs, because the die-offs seem necessary to the bamboo. Die-offs benefit giant pandas as well. They encourage diversity in breeding, because pandas have to migrate to new areas for new sources of food. "It

Clematis vine grows along with bamboo and evergreen trees at Wuyipeng in the Wolong Nature Reserve.

would be risky to meddle with relationships we do not fully understand," states the WWF report on the Ministry of Forestry's plan.

More Panda Land

Another popular project is the creation of 14 new panda reserves with 2,000 square miles (5,185 sq km) of land added to protected panda habitat. Some land where giant pandas do not live will be removed from the reserves, while other land that is panda habitat will become part of a reserve.

The Chinese plan also calls for the construction of 15 wilderness corridors linking the reserves. These will provide pathways that giant pandas can use to travel between the reserves. It would give them the opportunity to mingle with pandas of other populations. This would allow for less inbreeding and more genetic diversity. Giant pandas could also move to a new location more easily if the bamboo in their area flowered and died.

In order to create these corridors, trees and bamboo would have to be replanted in areas where they were cut down for logging, agriculture, and building. This process would cost about $20 million, and it would be years before the pandas could actually travel through the corridors. Some people doubt that the corridors can ever be successful,

Since only 12 percent of China's land area is forested, many Chinese have a hard time finding wood for their daily needs. Sometimes those living next to or within panda reserve areas are caught harvesting wood where it is not permitted (below). They are usually fined and released.

Scientists capture giant pandas so they can be moved to more suitable locations. A captured panda is usually weighed before it is transported.

because there is already too much damage to repair. But conservationists argue that creating the corridors is the most important thing that can be done to save giant pandas.

In the meantime, some scientists are considering a plan to capture a number of giant pandas and actually move them to new locations. Small populations of pandas would be rounded up and added to larger populations. Unfortunately, there has been little actual experience with moving giant pandas from one wilderness area to another. Studies have shown, however, that pandas do not adjust easily to new locations.

Changes in Forestry and Farming

New forestry methods are also necessary, according to the panda conservation plan. Since there is a severe lumber shortage in China, it is not possible to halt all logging in the pandas' forests. Still, logging must be done in a way that does not harm pandas. Selective cutting is one acceptable method.

In selective cutting, the wilderness is not completely destroyed. Bamboo is not cut down, and many trees are left. Seeds from the remaining trees can help the forest grow back. In addition, loggers leave behind some of the large, hollow trees in which giant panda mothers like to have their babies so that the birthing and rearing process can continue naturally.

Changes in agriculture are also necessary. Farmers living near panda forests cannot be allowed to grow crops ever higher up mountain slopes, destroying panda habitat as they go. Instead, compromises must be found so that the farmers can earn a living while still keeping land wild for pandas.

Chinese peasants, such as the one in the picture, can live in harmony with the panda as long as they are willing to use the land wisely so panda habitat is not destroyed.

The Chinese government has agreed to pay farmers who follow five rules: no fires on their land, no cutting trees, no hunting, no breaking of new ground, and no damage to forests that are being replanted. The problems come when officials do not strictly enforce the rules.

Forest guards are supposed to report and arrest people who do not follow the conservation rules. But the guards are often from the local area themselves. They realize the importance of building fires, cutting timber, hunting, and plowing in the lives of the peasants—these are things people do to survive. The guards sympathize with the lawbreakers and often overlook their misdeeds.

Pulling the Plug on Poaching

The Ministry of Forestry's panda conservation plan mentions the problems of poaching but makes no specific recommendations. And within the Chinese legal system, there are mixed messages.

In October 1987, the Chinese Supreme Court ruled that killing giant pandas or trading panda pelts could bring severe punishment, including life in prison and even death. In February 1988, the first life sentences were handed down for the killing of two pandas. In October 1989, two people became the first offenders executed for trading panda skins.

But though the laws are strict, enforcement is often slack. There are few patrols to seek out poachers, and little effort is made to get poachers to remove their snares from the panda forest. Many conservationists complain that police in the reserves are basically lazy. They make excuses for not doing their work. Reserve police, however, say they don't have time to watch over pandas. Government officials in Beijing have not been helpful in providing additional assistance.

Time Is Running Out

Clearly, the many problems surrounding pandas have no simple solution. All we know for sure is that whatever is done to save pandas must be done quickly. And we must worry not only about pandas but about their entire habitat.

The forests hold untold riches that the world cannot afford to lose. Many species of plants and animals in the forests have been used in traditional Chinese medicines for centuries. The gall bladder of the black bear, for example, was used to treat

The Sichuan panda forests are full of many species of plants and animals that are important not only for their beauty but for traditional Chinese medicines.

ulcers, burns, and fevers. Researchers are now finding that these plants and animals are keys to entirely new classes of drugs with the potential to cure many diseases. If the pandas' forests are lost forever, so are these important plants and animals.

The forest also helps prevent erosion on the mountainside. The roots of trees and shrubs hold soil in place, reducing the risk of droughts, floods, and mud slides.

With so much depending on these forests, people throughout the world must work together to save them. Solutions must be found.

"This fragile, ancient panda life-style will endure only for a few more years if pandas and their habitat are not protected immediately," wrote Hu Jinchu. "It is incumbent upon humankind to save the panda from extinction."

Jia Lin, a five-month-old giant panda, roams free in the Wolong forests of Sichuan.

GLOSSARY

artificial insemination – a technique in which sperm is extracted from a male animal and injected into a female in order to fertilize an egg.

clear-cutting – a method used to harvest a forest in which all trees in a section are cut down regardless of size, age, or quality.

conservation – reducing the use of natural resources by cutting down demand or by using those resources more efficiently.

ecosystem – a group of living organisms in a particular physical environment where the numbers and kinds of plants and animals remain stable or balanced.

encroachment – the taking over and development of wilderness areas by humans.

endangered species – a plant or animal that has so few living members that it may become extinct if it is not protected.

erosion – the wearing away of the Earth's surface by wind, water, or ice.

extinct – a plant or animal that once existed on Earth but no longer has any living members.

fragmentation – dividing habitat into small separate, disconnected segments by such things as clear-cutting, roads, farming, or development.

gene – a unit of heredity made of DNA, usually a protein that controls the transmission of a trait in a plant or animal.

habitat – the physical environment in which a plant or animal lives.

humus – dead plant and animal tissues that are partly or entirely decomposed; a dark brown material that enriches the soil.

inbreeding – mating between family members who carry similar genes. It tends to decrease the vitality of a species.

lichens – plants made up of an alga and fungus living together.

mammals – any warm-blooded vertebrate animal, usually with hair or fur, that feeds its young with mother's milk.

natural reserves – parcels of land set aside by governments to preserve wilderness areas and the animals living in them.

niche – a habitat that supports the unique functions of a specific plant or animal.

predator – an animal that hunts and kills other animals for food.

selective cutting – a method used in harvesting a forest in which only the mature or selected trees are cut.

species – the smallest unit in categorizing living organisms; those that are related and can interbreed with each other.

territory – the area over which an individual animal ranges and which it may defend from others of the same species.

topsoil – the upper layer of earth, containing many of the nutrients needed to support healthy plant growth.

wilderness corridors – strips of undeveloped land linking wilderness areas.

FOR MORE INFORMATION

Books

Bailey, Jill. *Project Panda*. "Save Our Species" series. Austin, Tex.: Raintree Steck-Vaughn, 1990.

Bright, Michael. *Giant Panda*. New York: Gloucester, 1989.

Catton, Chris. *Pandas*. New York: Facts on File, 1990.

Green, Carl R. *The Giant Panda*. Mankato, Minn.: Crestwood House, 1987.

Harkness, Ruth. *The Lady and the Panda*. New York: Carrick & Evans, 1938.

Irvine, Georgeane. *The Visit of Two Giant Pandas at the San Diego Zoo*. New York: Simon & Schuster Books for Young Readers, 1991.

McClung, Robert M. *Li-Li, A Giant Panda of Sichuan*. New York: Morrow Junior Books, 1988.

Morris, Ramona and Morris, Desmond. *Men and Pandas*. New York: McGraw-Hill, 1966.

Perry, Richard. *The World of the Giant Panda*. New York: Taplinger, 1969.

Preiss, Byron and Gao Xueyu, editors. *The Secret World of Pandas*. New York: Abrams, 1990.

Rau, Margaret. *The Giant Panda at Home*. New York: Knopf, 1977.

Rogers, Barbara Radcliffe. *Giant Pandas*. New York: Mallard Press, 1990.

Roots, Clive. *The Bamboo Bears*. Winnipeg, Canada: Hyperion, 1989.

Schaller, George B. *The Last Panda*. Chicago: University of Chicago, 1993.

Schaller, George B., Hu Jinchu, Pan Wenshi, and Zhu Jing. *The Giant Pandas of Wolong*. Chicago: University of Chicago, 1985.

Periodicals

"Bamboo Breakthrough." *National Geographic World*, Vol. 183, pp. 10-11, November 1990.

Dolnick, E. "Panda Paradox." *Discover*, Vol. 10, pp. 70-74, September 1989.

Lu Zhi, "Newborn Panda in the Wild." *National Geographic*, Vol. 183, pp. 60-65, February 1993.

Schaller, George B. "Pandas in the Wild." *National Geographic*, Vol. 160, pp. 735-749, December 1981.

Shipman, P. "Killer Bamboo." *Discover*, Vol. 11, p. 22, February 1990.

VIDEOS AND CASSETTES

American Adventure Productions. *Struggle to Survive: China's Giant Panda*. MPI Home Video, 1991.

Beishung: the Giant Panda. Chicago: Society for Visual Education, 1978. (Cassette)

The Panda: With Love from China. Horizon Entertainment Group in association with Chanco Entertainment Group, 1989.

INDEX